vjbnf   VAL
791.84 ABDO

Abdo, Kenny, 1986- author
Rodeos
33410015356191   06/12/19

C0-DYE-483

Valparaiso Public Library
103 Jefferson Street
Valparaiso, IN 46383

ARENA EVENTS
RODEOS

Fly!
An Imprint of Abdo Zoom
abdobooks.com

KENNY ABDO

abdobooks.com

Published by Abdo Zoom, a division of ABDO, P.O. Box 398166, Minneapolis, Minnesota 55439. Copyright © 2019 by Abdo Consulting Group, Inc. International copyrights reserved in all countries. No part of this book may be reproduced in any form without written permission from the publisher. Fly!™ is a trademark and logo of Abdo Zoom.

Printed in the United States of America, North Mankato, Minnesota.
092018
012019

Photo Credits: Everette Collection, iStock, Shutterstock
Production Contributors: Kenny Abdo, Jennie Forsberg, Grace Hansen
Design Contributors: Dorothy Toth, Neil Klinepier

Library of Congress Control Number: 2018946206

Publisher's Cataloging-in-Publication Data

Names: Abdo, Kenny, author.
Title: Rodeos / by Kenny Abdo.
Description: Minneapolis, Minnesota : Abdo Zoom, 2019 | Series: Arena events | Includes online resources and index.
Identifiers: ISBN 9781532125386 (lib. bdg.) | ISBN 9781641856829 (pbk) | ISBN 9781532126406 (ebook) | ISBN 9781532126918 (Read-to-me ebook)
Subjects: LCSH: Rodeo events--Juvenile literature. | Rodeo performers--Juvenile literature. | Rodeo animals--Juvenile literature.
Classification: DDC 791.84--dc23

TABLE OF CONTENTS

Rodeos 4

Opening Act 8

The Main Event 16

Glossary 22

Online Resources 23

Index 24

RODEOS

Bucking into arenas from the Americas to Europe, Rodeos have audience members on the edge of their seats!

The sport comes from **techniques** cowboys use on the ranch to round-up cattle.

Rodeo comes from the Spanish word *rodear*. It means "to round-up." The skills of early Spanish **cattle drivers** were taught to American cowboys after the **Civil War**.

The first recorded rodeo was held in Arizona in 1864. "Buffalo Bill" Cody organized the first U.S. rodeo and Wild West show in Nebraska in 1882.

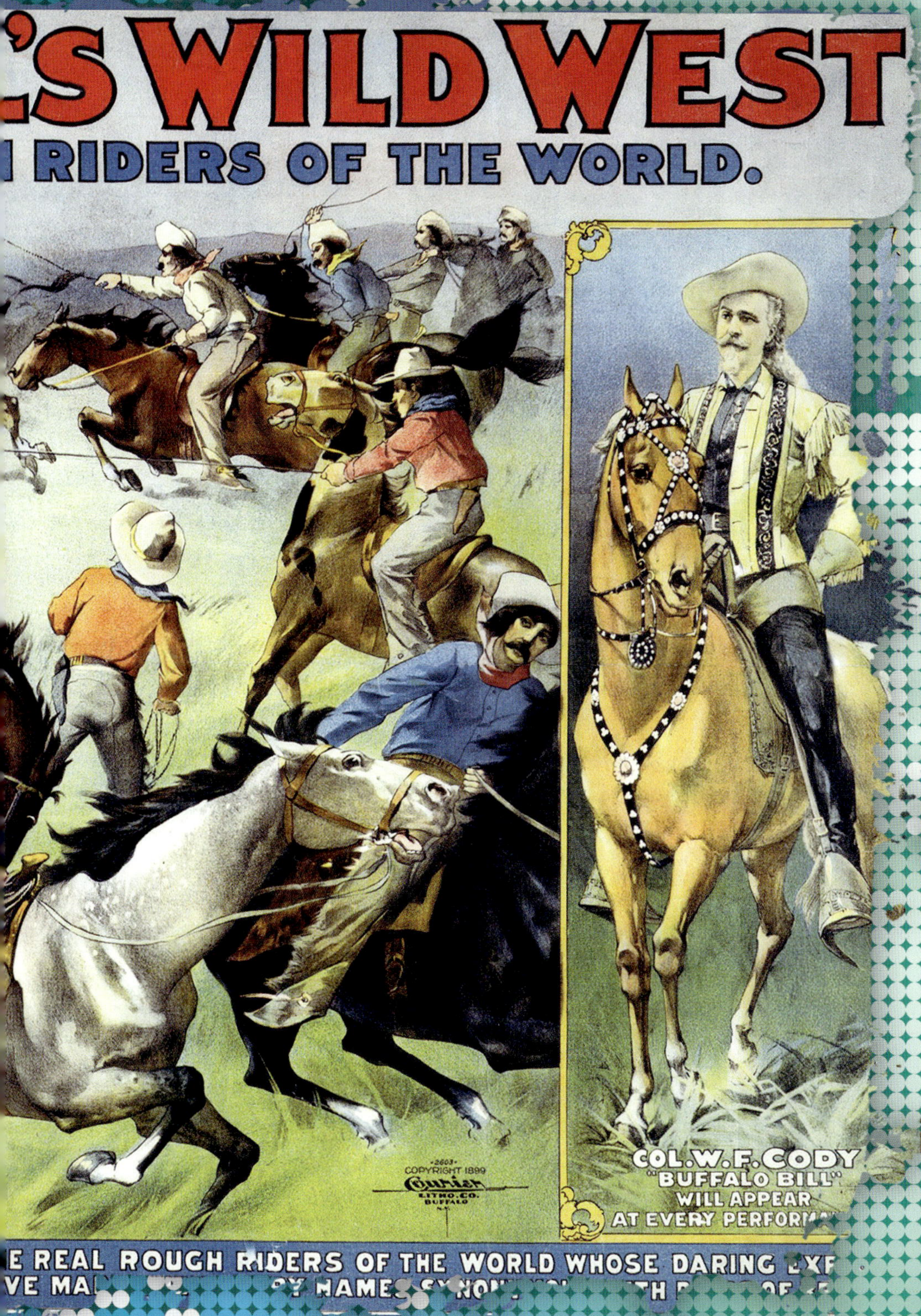
'S WILD WEST
RIDERS OF THE WORLD.
COPYRIGHT 1899
Courier
LITHO. CO.
BUFFALO
COL. W. F. CODY
"BUFFALO BILL"
WILL APPEAR
AT EVERY PERFORM
E REAL ROUGH RIDERS OF THE WORLD WHOSE DARING EXP

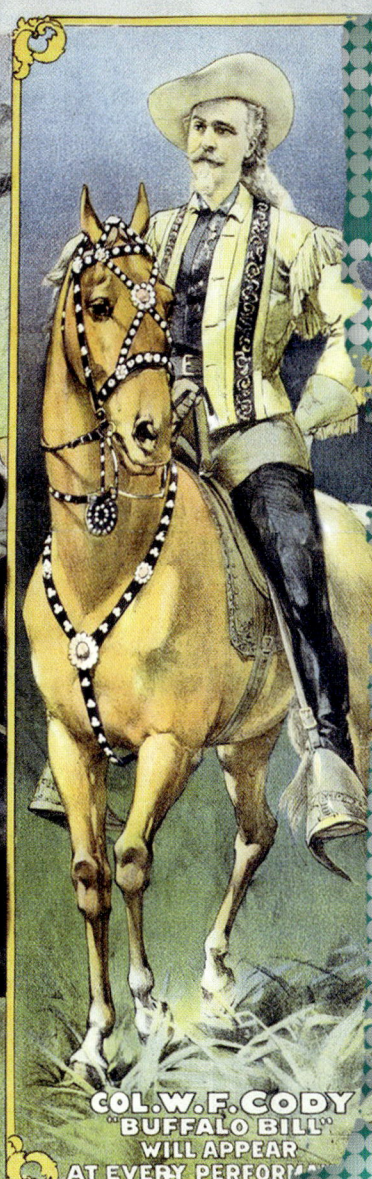

Today's rodeos are broken up into many **events**. Some include Calf Roping, **Bareback** Riding, and Saddle Bronc Riding. Professional Bull Riding and Steer Wrestling are other popular events.

Rodeo clowns are highly-skilled athletes. Their job is to distract the bull when a cowboy falls so they can escape unharmed.

THE MAIN EVENT

Rodeos are the official state sport of Texas and Wyoming. Professional Bull Riding is the most popular **event**.

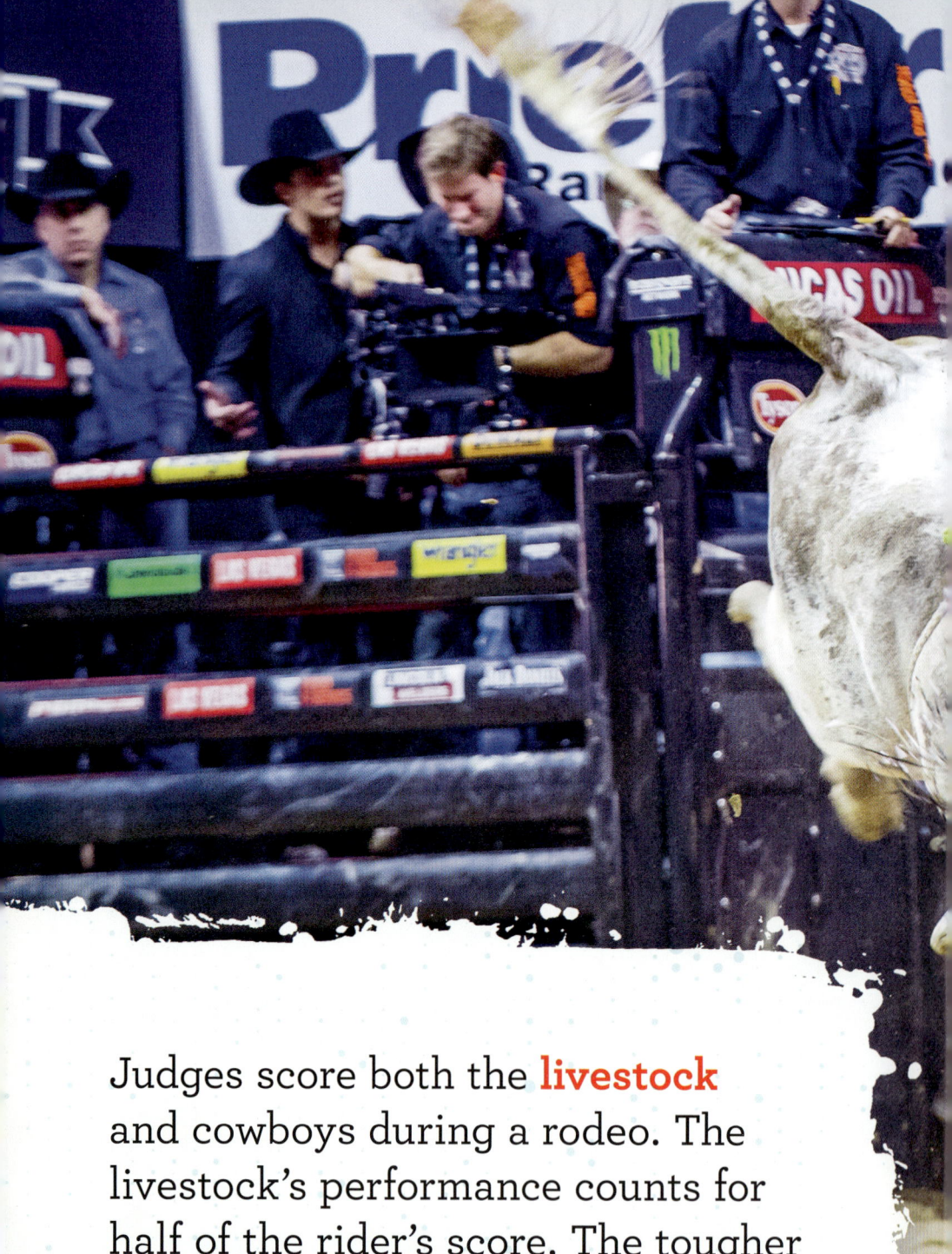

Judges score both the **livestock** and cowboys during a rodeo. The livestock's performance counts for half of the rider's score. The tougher the ride, the higher the total. The perfect score is 100 points.

There are two kinds of animals at rodeos: those owned by the cowboys and those that are from a stock **supplier**. Cowboys bring their own horses if they are in an **event** like Roping. If they are in a bucking event, they ride a supplied horse.

GLOSSARY

bareback – to be on an unsaddled animal.

cattle driver – someone who moves a herd of cattle from one place to another.

Civil War – a war between the United States of America and the Confederate States of America fought from 1861 to 1865.

event – one part that makes up a sports competition.

livestock – animals that a farmer owns.

supplier – a group that provides something needed.

technique – a method or style in which something is done.

ONLINE RESOURCES

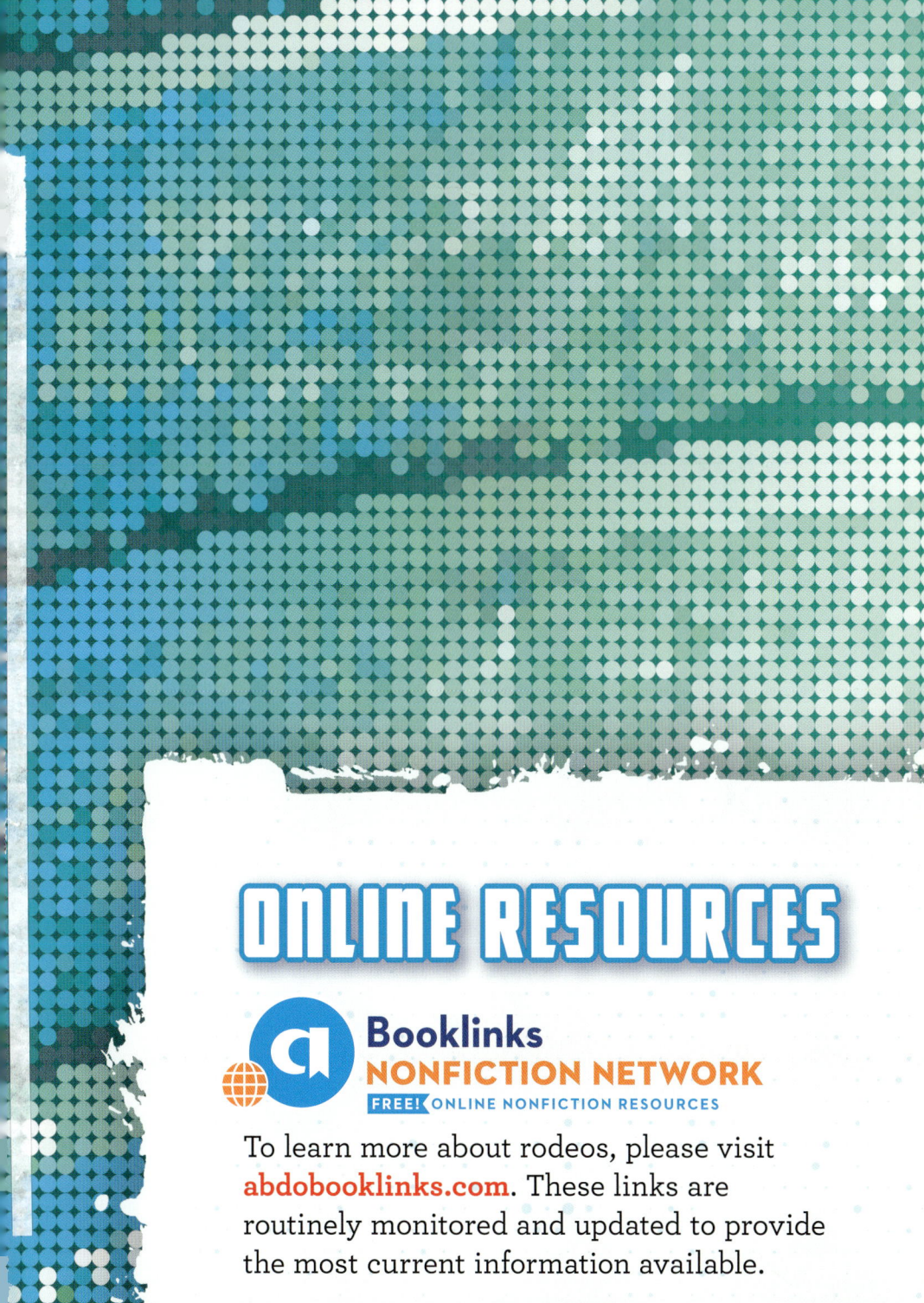

Booklinks
NONFICTION NETWORK
FREE! ONLINE NONFICTION RESOURCES

To learn more about rodeos, please visit **abdobooklinks.com**. These links are routinely monitored and updated to provide the most current information available.

Americas 4

Arizona 10

Civil War 9

Cody, Bill 10

cowboys 7, 9, 14

Europe 4

events 13, 16, 21

judging 18

Nebraska 10

origins 7, 9, 10

rodeo clowns 14

Texas 16

Wyoming 16